D1361081

We've Got to Stop Meeting Like This!

Meeting Management for Leaders and Participants

George Lowe and Tony Jeary

Novations Training Solutions, Inc.
4621 121ST Street
Urbandale IA, 50323
1-888-776-8268
www.novationstraining.com

We've Got to Stop Meeting Like This!
Meeting Management for Leaders and Participants

George Lowe and Tony Jeary
Copyright © 2000 by George Lowe and Tony Jeary

Novations Training Solutions, Inc.
Project Manager: Todd McDonald
Designer: Gayle O'Brien

Published by Novations Training Solutions, Inc.
4621 121ST Street
Urbandale IA, 50323
1-800-262-2557

Library of Congress Catalog Card Number 00-105695
Lowe, George and Jeary, Tony
We've Got to Stop Meeting Like This!

Printed in the United States of America
2000
ISBN 1-884926-09-6

Why You Should Read This Book

If you answer *yes* to any of the following questions, then the ideas contained in this book can save you time and money and help your team or organization become more effective.

Check all that apply:

1. Do you believe that meetings frequently are not a good use of your time? Have you said to yourself, "Why am I here?" _____

2. Do you work with people who are not sensitive to the costs related to meetings? _____

3. Have you ever felt trapped in a meeting room? Have you filled your note pad with doodles out of boredom? Is lack of focus or digression from the subject a problem in the meetings you attend? _____

4. Have you attended a meeting recently that created more problems than it solved? _____

5. Does your team have trouble reaching agreement during a meeting or sustaining the agreement after the meeting? Have you had to repeat a meeting because the true decision-makers weren't in the room and didn't buy in to the agreements reached? _____

6. Have you ever found it hard to get a word in edgewise, or felt like putting a gag on someone who dominated a meeting? _____

7. Are you weary of preparing for meetings only to find someone reading the same material to you from the podium? Are you tired of people who don't prepare for your meetings? _____

8. Do you recognize that meetings can be a great showcase for leadership and management talents? _____

9. Are you tired of squinting at slides that can't be read from the back of the room and/or illegible handwriting on flip-charts? _____

10. Do you and your team spend a lot of time in meetings (and would you like to spend less time while accomplishing more)? _____

About the Authors

Tony Jeary

Tony Jeary—Mr. Presentation™ is one of the country's best-known authors, coaches and presenters on presentation skills and making the most out of your time in front of people. He is the author or co-author of eight highly-acclaimed books along with several popular workshops and video programs. He serves as coach and seminar leader for Fortune 100 corporations and organizations around the world.

Combined with the success of his debut book, *Inspire Any Audience*, his books have sold more than 75,000 copies. His latest work is a co-authorship with Dr. Robert Rohm entitled, *Presenting with Style*. Additional titles include, *Nervous to Natural*, *The Complete Guide to Effective Facilitation*, *Training Other People to Train*, *Ice Breakers*, *Activities and Attention Keepers* and, a personal favorite, *The Good Sense Guide to Happiness*.

Tony and his wife, Tammy have been married for ten years and have two daughters who are powerful presenters in their own right.

You can reach Tony at 877-2-INSPIRE or www.MrPresentation.com.

George Lowe

George Lowe has spent over thirty-five years in the automotive business with one of the big three manufacturers and has developed meeting management techniques for use by his teams and others in a wide variety of settings.

He has held leadership positions in Marketing, Sales, Service, Product Development and Quality in the U.S. and Mexico, and has led global organizations and numerous cross-functional teams.

His meeting management process understanding is founded on years of study and real-world experience in leading and participating in thousands of meetings. The concepts contained in this book have been validated in a wide array of work settings in both non-technical and technical functions.

You can reach George via e-mail at: georgelowe@ameritech.net

● Table of Contents

Chapter *One*

Knowing What Success Looks Like

Chapter Objectives

▶ Recognize why you should be concerned about managing meetings.

▶ Explain what it takes to have good meetings.

▶ Recognize when you should call a meeting and when you should consider other methods to accomplish the goal.

▶ Build the case for change in your organization.

Why Should You Care About Meetings?

Is running an effective meeting really that important to your success and the success of your organization? The answer is yes! There are many reasons why you should be concerned about the quality and effectiveness of your meetings. Here are just a few of them.

"It is not necessary to change. Survival is not mandatory."
W. Edwards Deming

Making the Most of Time

Time is at a premium for all professionals today, and many of us will spend as much as half of our work hours in meetings. Many senior executives clock *more than 40 hours a week* in meetings, leaving little time for anything else. Accordingly:

◆ Reductions in the number and/or length of meetings is a high-leverage time saver.

◆ Just a 10 percent reduction in time spent in meetings would result in substantial savings for the organization and/or offer an important improvement in the quality of work life.

Sharing Diverse Views

Organizations can benefit from creative ideas and diverse views only when those ideas and views are shared. Good meeting management can improve the communication process and help all views get a fair hearing.

Improving Productivity

Doing more with less is the standard for today's organizations. Meetings can be a significant source of productivity improvement when you consider that:

Meetings can be a significant source of productivity improvement .

◆ At least one third of all meetings are considered unnecessary or unproductive by some attendees.

◆ Virtually all meetings are perceived as having some unproductive segments.

◆ Attention to just the rudimentary elements of meeting management can save hours, especially when you consider the multiplier effect of the number of people in given meetings.

Building Credibility and Image

Valuable, efficient, and effective meetings can be major contributors to the leader's professional success. By providing a focused view of their skills, talents and knowledge, meeting leaders can demonstrate to senior managers or key customers that they are ready for more challenging assignments.

On the other hand, poorly handled meetings can destroy an individual's reputation and credibility, and be career (or organization) killers—not only for the meeting leader but also for associates.

> "Until you value yourself, you won't value your time. Until you value your time, you will not do anything with it."
> **M. Scott Peck**

Respecting Others' Time

An important underlying value that drives the need for disciplined meeting management is the concept that time is a scarce, costly resource.

◆ For many, time has become *more* valuable than money, and people's attitude about how to use time has become much more protective.

◆ Wasting significant amounts of someone's time is tantamount to putting your hand in that person's wallet. Moreover, you may get people to waste their time once in an ineffective meeting, but it's unlikely that you'll be able to get them to attend another.

Take a Moment

Can you think of any other reasons why effectively managing meetings is important? List them below.

_____

_____

_____

Determining Whether a Meeting Is Required

Many meetings get off to a bad start because they involved the wrong set of people, were called at the wrong time, or shouldn't have been called at all. Before calling a meeting, consider the following:

Results Needed

Think about what specific outcome or results are needed before calling a meeting to ensure that there isn't a better method for accomplishing the task.

Type of Work

Groups are not well suited for some kinds of work (writing and editing, for example)—delegate these tasks to individuals.

Costs

Meetings can be very costly. Consider some of the costs associated with gathering a specific group of people—their salaries, lost sales or production time, travel and lodging, etc.

Always ask yourself whether the potential benefits of what you want to accomplish justify the costs.

Alternative Methods

Here are a few alternative methods that can be more efficient and effective than traditional face-to-face meetings for certain tasks:

- ◆ Conference calls

- ◆ Web- or LAN-based on-line meetings

- ◆ Videotaped messages

- ◆ Paper or e-mail bulletins with response mechanisms

- ◆ Studies conducted by individuals

- ◆ Documents created collaboratively

Many of the above can be good alternatives for face-to-face meetings, or can provide background so that meetings can be shorter and more productive.

> **"There is nothing so useless as doing efficiently that which should not be done at all."**
> **Peter Drucker**

Take a Moment

Think of a meeting you recently attended that seemed ineffective. Could the same goals have been accomplished more effectively using one of the alternative methods just described. Which alternative do you think would have been most effective, and why?

_____

_____

_____

Building Your Meeting Management System

When a meeting is required, you can help ensure it's effective by working to build meeting management skills throughout your organization. Like any other goal worth pursuing, this will require commitment and discipline on the part of meeting leaders and participants. Rome wasn't built in a day, and building an organization's meeting management skills isn't a one-step, overnight process. Here are the foundations for creating an effective meeting management system:

Building an organization's meeting management skills isn't a one-step, overnight process.

Reaching Critical Mass

Even though the basics of meeting management can be taught quickly (in five minutes or less if you are pressed), you need to have a sufficient number of participants who know how to—and want to—play the game in order to move past an elementary level.

If you're a supervisor or manager, you can gather critical mass faster by mandating a trial of meeting management techniques. If you're not the boss, you can still recruit others to help demonstrate the benefits of good meetings.

Offering Clear Leadership

Not all participants will immediately see the value and benefits of improved meetings:

◆ Some may find the mechanical aspects of good meetings unduly bureaucratic.

◆ Others may feel threatened by the higher standards for discipline and preparation that are implied.

But even though some team members may have misgivings, their conditional support is needed to make meeting management work. This is where the support of management becomes especially important. While senior people don't have to be the source of the idea, they must buy in to the goals of meeting management to provide support and advocacy during the early days.

Supporting Flexibility and Creativity

Meeting processes require constant tailoring to respond to the needs of organizers and participants, to respond to the challenges of everyday business conditions, and to take advantage of opportunities that emerge.

> Meeting processes require constant tailoring to respond to the needs of organizers and participants.

◆ People skilled in meeting management develop a sense of how to balance time, participation, and creative digression to achieve desired outcomes, and sometimes may violate literal "rules" in order to get the job done.

◆ "Meeting police" who rigidly enforce structural rules while sacrificing results can ruin meeting management for everyone by giving discipline a bad name.

Next Steps—Starting a Meeting Management Movement

Getting started begins with your understanding of the case for change in your organization and your ability to recruit others to support your efforts. When you finish studying the material in this book, you should be in position to develop a case for change tailored to your organization.

Self-Check Chapter One Review

Now that you've read Chapter One, use this space to review what you've learned so far. If you're not sure, refer back to the text. Answers appear on page 101.

1. Just a _____ percent reduction in time spent in meetings would result in substantial savings for organizations and improved work life for employees.

2. For many in the workplace today, time has become _____ valuable than money.

3. List four things you should consider when determining whether or not a meeting is required.

   _____

   _____

   _____

   _____

4. What are three alternatives to a face-to-face meeting?

   _____

   _____

   _____

5. What does "critical mass" mean in relation to meeting management?

_____

_____

_____

_____

1

6. Why are "meeting police" poor meeting leaders?

_____

_____

_____

_____

Chapter *Two*

Preparation Pays

Chapter Objectives

▶ Explain why preparation is important.

▶ Explore the central importance of a clear purpose and desired outcomes—the *what* and *why* questions.

▶ Understand the importance of carefully selecting participants—the *who* questions.

▶ Practice building a timed agenda, including the key *how, when* and *how long* questions.

▶ Develop the idea of prework--things that can speed the meeting by being done ahead of time.

Preparation Is Important

Because of busy schedules, meeting leaders and participants may be tempted to devote little time to meeting preparation. But skilled meeting leaders know that preparation is the most important phase of the meeting management process. They recognize that prep time should usually equal or exceed the time devoted to the actual meeting.

> **Preparation is the most important phase of the meeting management process.**

If this sounds like too much effort, remember that preparation costs incurred by an individual or small group can be quickly offset when a meeting involving a large group can be shortened or made more effective.

You can begin to prepare for a meeting by answering these basic questions:

◆ *Why* are you holding the meeting?

◆ *What* do you want to accomplish?

◆ *Who* should participate?

◆ *How* should you conduct the meeting?

◆ *When* should you hold the meeting, and how long should it take?

Defining *Why* and *What* Is Vital

If you don't have a clear purpose for the meeting (the answer to "Why are we here?"), you immediately risk wasting time and limiting accomplishments.

Similarly, participants want to know the answer to the *what* questions, such as "*What* are we trying to accomplish?" and "*What* are we going to review/talk about?" A clear *purpose statement* with *desired outcomes* to match will go a long way toward ensuring a productive meeting.

Participants want to know the answers to the *what* and *why* questions.

◆ *Purpose statements* are short, punchy phrases that typically describe the functional or subject matter content of a meeting.

◆ *Desired outcomes* statements are longer and more specific— they contain action words that describe the actual work to be done during the session.

Placement of Desired Outcomes on the Agenda

◆ List desired outcomes near the top of the page or next to topics.

◆ The desired outcomes must match the overall meeting purpose, the capabilities of the group, and the time available.

List desired outcomes near the top of the page or next to topics.

On the next page are some sample purpose statements with matching desired outcomes.

Purpose Statement	Desired Outcomes Statements
Monthly sales reviews	• Learn prior month's sales results and celebrate successes. • Discuss accounts with below-objective year-to-date purchases and develop action plans. • Develop/agree on plans for special sales actions for next month. • Come to consensus on forecast for next month. • Review marketing support for fourth quarter. • Learn sales tip of the month.
Purpose Statement	**Desired Outcomes Statements**

Spring recruiting planning session	• Identify new college graduate personnel hiring needs.
	• Discuss/confirm colleges and universities targeted for on-campus recruiting.
	    - Understand last year's results.
	    - Suggest adds and deletes.
	• Identify materials needed for advance solicitation of candidates.
	• Identify/assign on-campus recruiters.
	• Outline work plans--who does what by when?

Take a Moment

Write a purpose statement and one or more desired
outcomes statements for a meeting you have coming up.

Purpose   *Desired Outcome(s)*

_____   _____

_____   _____

_____

_____

_____

_____

_____

_____

2

Determining *Who* Should Participate

Determining *who* is needed to accomplish meeting goals
(and ensuring that key people will attend) is as important as
determining the meeting topic. Consider the following when
building your invitation list:

> **Determining
> who is needed
> to accomplish
> meeting goals
> is as important
> as determining
> the meeting
> topic.**

Content Contributors

◆ Decision-makers, front-line people, and subject matter
   experts can be important contributors/participants in a
   meeting.

◆ Any of these groups alone may not understand the issues
   completely, and/or may not be empowered to act.

Process Contributors

♦ Meeting process experts (facilitator, recorder, etc.) often can make substantial contributions even without subject matter or functional expertise by providing unbiased facilitation and/or by freeing up the meeting leaders to actively participate.

♦ Exercise care in retaining this kind of support—outsiders must use techniques your group can work with and adapt to your needs. Don't hire meeting police.

How Many Should Attend?

If you have too few people, an inappropriate mix of people, or some with insufficient background or authority in the room, you may not achieve your desired outcomes, or you may need to take substantial post-meeting action to achieve buy-in and fill gaps. Depending on who is missing, there can be a risk of total rework.

Inviting too many people with redundant representation of various points of view can risk wholesale time wasting. Judgment is required here. In some cases you'll want or need "everyone" in order to assure participation and/or buy-in; other times "everyone" may feel like the work could have been accomplished by a much smaller group, and you'll lose support because of the perception of wasted time.

The size of the group creates significant constraints on the effectiveness of two-way communication.

The size of the group creates significant constraints on the effectiveness of two-way communication. Generally speaking, smaller is better if a high degree of interaction is needed. On the next page are some guidelines on size-related matters:

Group Size	Characteristics and Limitations	
Small (Up to 10-15 people)	• Can be highly interactive, and flexible in terms of content and pacing; can move very fast when motivated by subject matter or a skilled facilitator.	• Break-out groups or table groups generally aren't practical or desirable in groups of less than 10 unless there are very logical segments within the group.
Medium (15-40)	• Interaction, two-way communication is possible; skilled facilitation is required to assure full participation. • Less flexible than small groups in terms of content and pacing.	• Requires more time to cover same material (with full participation). • May require the use of table groups or break-out groups to gather and focus input efficiently.
Large (40-100)	• Interaction and two-way communication are difficult; skilled facilitation is required to assure representative participation. • Less flexible than smaller groups in terms of content and pacing—stick to the agenda.	• Requires a lot of time to cover same material with participation, especially if the subject is controversial. • Requires the use of table or break-out groups to gather and focus input efficiently.
Very Large (100-500) and **Huge** (500 and up)	• Interaction and two-way communication are very limited and require special structure (think of political conventions). • Skilled facilitation is required to ensure representative participation. • Highly inflexible relative to content and pacing—audience will leave if they're bored or if the meeting goes off track.	• Requires a lot of time to cover substantive material—prereading assignments are mandatory if accurate feedback is needed. • Table or break-out groups are impractical and logistically difficult. • Overnight or lunchtime caucuses and/or paper polls can sometimes be used to gather opinions efficiently.

2

Planning the *How*

Planning which methods and techniques to use in conducting the meeting can help you reach desired outcomes and get the most out of the participant group. Following are some of the methods that can be used along with characteristics and typical applications:

Methods	Applications and Characteristics
Presentation	• Used for straightforward presentation of data or information when discussion or Q&A is not needed or desired. • Generally used for factual, noncontroversial subject matter (statistical data such as sales or production results, for example).
Present & Discuss	• Used for presentation of data or information when discussion or Q&A is needed to assure understanding or to achieve buy-in. • Generally used for subject matter that may be open to interpretation or that is tentative in nature. (analysis of research results, proposed advertising plans, quality issues, etc.)
Q&A new	• Similar to discussion but used when subject matter is not tentative and when the expert is on stage to answer questions, clarifying or interpreting material presented (e.g.presenting the performance appraisal system).
Brainstorm	• Used in situations where lists of things (ideas, concepts, solutions to problems, etc.) need to be generated. • With medium and larger group sizes, needs to be done in break-out or table groups

continued on the next page

22

Methods	Applications and Characteristics
Consolidate	• Used to clean-up results of brainstorming by consolidating similar/related items. • As with brainstorming, with medium and larger group sizes, initial consolidations need to be done in break-out or table groups.
Order/Prioritize	• Used to sequence and organize results of brainstorming/consolidation.
Develop	• Used to build solutions, work plans, and timetables.
Agree	• Usually used in conjunction with or following present & discuss items to reach consensus and closure on an action plan.
Evaluate	• Used for rating segments--for evaluation of task content or meeting processes.
Recap	• Used by the meeting/topic leader to confirm achievement of outcomes and support of work plans, timetables, etc. • Also may be used at the beginning of meetings to provide recaps of a previous session on the same subject.

2

Take a Moment

List three methods from the above table that you haven't used regularly and think about how you might use them in future meetings:

1. _____

2. _____

3. _____

Deciding *When*, and *How Long*

Selecting when—date and time—to conduct a meeting can be important. Consider your desired outcomes and their time sensitivity as well as the availability of key stakeholders when scheduling your meeting. Time of day can impact your outcomes as well. Many people don't do well in meetings right after lunch or at the end of the workday. The day of the week or month can be important as well. If your organization has exceptionally busy days, try to avoid these as your participants may be distracted or simply not available.

Timing Is Critical

Time allocation is key to getting maximum outputs in minimum time:

◆ Realistic estimates can be based on experience or prework (rehearsal, opinion sampling, etc.).

◆ Be conservative—finishing early is almost always okay.

◆ If you do time allocations right, about one quarter of participants will say, "We wish we had more time for _____," while the bulk of the attendees will be pleased with the efficiency.

◆ The facilitator (if different from the meeting leader) must understand and agree to the time budget for the session. Build in some time flexibility for his or her use during the meeting.

◆ If more time is needed to achieve desired outcomes or buy-in, the group needs to be asked about extensions and trade-offs.

◆ To either extend or cut off without group agreement is rude and can destroy potential accomplishments.

◆ Extensions that blow the scheduled end-time for the meeting are particularly critical. People have commitments—airplanes, other meetings, family needs—that may not be ignored without serious consequences. Meeting leaders that routinely run over are remembered in an unfavorable light.

Teleconferencing, Videoconferencing, and Web Meetings

We won't directly cover teleconferencing, videoconferencing, and Web meetings because the same principles that apply to face-to-face sessions apply to technology-enabled sessions. These methods offer substantial advantages in terms of increasing speed, reduced travel, and improved collaboration without regard to the location of participants.

2

However, the skilled meeting leader will recognize that these methods also have limitations, and compensate for the loss of face-to-face interaction to the extent possible. Some of considerations follow:

◆ Agendas and desired outcomes, published in advance, are even more important in an electronic meeting than in live forums. Participants can tune out if they aren't on the same page as the rest of the group regarding the purpose of the session.

◆ Networking with key players before the meeting also can improve results, by identifying issues and positions more clearly and dealing with specific concerns proactively.

◆ As body language is not available to send cues to the facilitator, verbal check-ins are needed on a more frequent basis.

◆ Technology-enabled meetings work best with people that already know each other, and know the subject matter. If a series of meetings is needed, an investment in a face-to-face kickoff meeting may be money well spent.

Final Tips

We've seen a number of ways that meeting leaders and participants can prepare for a meeting. Though it takes time, preparation pays off in terms of meeting productivity and efficiency. Here are some final suggestions:

Action	Content	Benefits
1. Send advance notices.	Distribute invitation/meeting notice well in advance; ask for RSVPs if appropriate. Include: • Agenda and list of participants. • Preparations expected of participants. • Materials (reading, work plans, status reports, etc.) required in advance. • Meeting role assignments (facilitator, recorder, etc.). Ask individuals to study/plan/rehearse as needed.	People are informed and have the material necessary to be prepared
2. Verify facilities, materials, and equipment.	Assess facilities, material and equipment needed to conduct the meeting and make necessary arrangements. Consider the following: • Room size, configuration and seating layout. • Food/beverage service (for lengthy sessions). • Break-out rooms (for sub-group work if needed). • Name tags and place cards. • Audio/visual equipment—phone lines for computer connections, etc. (It's important to functionally check these items and have spare bulbs/tapes etc. on hand).	Your space is right for the task at hand and there are no surprises at meeting time

2

Action	Content	Benefits
	• Agendas, handouts and reference materials (extra copies for those that don't bring their pre-read; revised agendas to cover late changes, etc.). • Note paper and writing instruments • Projectors, VCRs, PA system, lecterns.	
3. Plan for documentation.	1. Determine the degree of post-meeting documentation required: • Simple notes for participants. • "Group memory" (transcribed flipchart highlights). • Detailed minutes. • Summary findings/conclusion. • Work plans. • Video or audio recordings etc. • Verbatim records. 2. Plan for material/equipment needed to achieve documentation desired: • Flipcharts or electronic easel with appropriate markers. • Laptop word processor. • Tape recorder or video camcorder. • Court recorder for verbatim record.	You're ready to go at meeting time, and you don't have to draft a recorder at the last-minute.

Self-Check: Chapter Two Review

Answers to the following questions appear on pages 101 and 102.

1. What five basic questions should you answer before you begin preparing for your meeting?

   1. _____

   2. _____

   3. _____

   4. _____

   5. _____

2. Complete the following sentences:
   Purpose statements are short, punchy phrases that typically describe the _____ _____ content of a meeting.

   Desired outcomes statements are longer and more specific— they describe the _____ _____ to be done during the session.

3. True or False?
   Generally speaking, a smaller group size is better if a high degree of interaction is needed.

4. List three methods/techniques you can use when conducting a meeting.

   1. _____

   2. _____

   3. _____

5. Where should you list *desired outcomes* in a meeting agenda?

   _____

   _____

   _____

   _____

6. When do technology-enabled meetings work best?

   _____

   _____

   _____

   _____

2

Chapter *Three*
Layout Counts

Chapter Objectives

▶ Picking a meeting room that suits your purpose.

▶ Understanding the characteristics and limitations of various meeting room layouts.

Why the Meeting Room Is Important

The physical characteristics of meeting spaces can impact meetings.

Skilled meeting leaders know that the physical characteristics of their meeting space can impact their meetings. Whenever possible, experienced meeting organizers select a location based on the needs of the session. And when meeting leaders cannot choose the location, but must instead work within the constraints of an assigned meeting area, they use their knowledge of meeting spaces to adapt to the available room.

This chapter reviews several typical meeting layouts and identifies some of the characteristics, advantages, and limitations of each. The list is not exhaustive, however, and you'll find many variations on these themes. The table below includes key factors that you'll want to consider in selecting a place for an important meeting.

Factor	Sample Considerations
Group Size	• Meeting rooms should not be too large or too small—if you have to err on one side, meeting in a small room is often better than rattling around in wide open spaces. If you are faced with a room that is too large, bring people together in one end or corner.
Location	• Meeting participants do not enjoy having to drive or fly to a place that is viewed as inconvenient.
Interaction	• Interaction between the meeting leader and participants is increasingly difficult with groups of 25 and up; careful layout selection can mitigate these issues for some kinds of work.
Control	• Degree of control for the facilitator or meeting leader varies widely based on layouts and group size. Choose layouts very carefully for controversial or difficult subject matter.
Power	• Power balance among participants can be significantly affected by layout and seating. Understanding the power relationships associated with various seating arrangements can help you avoid surprises in meeting behaviors and outcomes.
Media	• Visual media (slide presentations, videos, overheads, flip charts) all come with limitations relative to sight lines and sight distances. A common error in meeting management involves the use of media that can't be seen by many participants.

3

continued on next page

Factor	Sample Considerations
Privacy & Quiet	• The "walls have ears" holds true in many meeting facilities. If you're dealing with sensitive or confidential material, find a place with good isolation.
	• Similarly, if you want your group to concentrate on it's work, you can't be in a room next door to a loud celebration or backed up to a busy kitchen.
Availability	• You will sometimes be forced to take the location that's available. In the authors' experience, these "sites" have included the hoods of cars, tailgates of trucks, and many a hallway and hotel lobby. A skilled leader is flexible enough to deal with any environment if no better spot is available.

Take a Moment

As you go through the next several pages of meeting room layouts, note, in the corner of the page, facilities that you have been in that are similar. Look at the characteristics and see if they tie with your experience.

Working with Typical Layouts

U-Shape

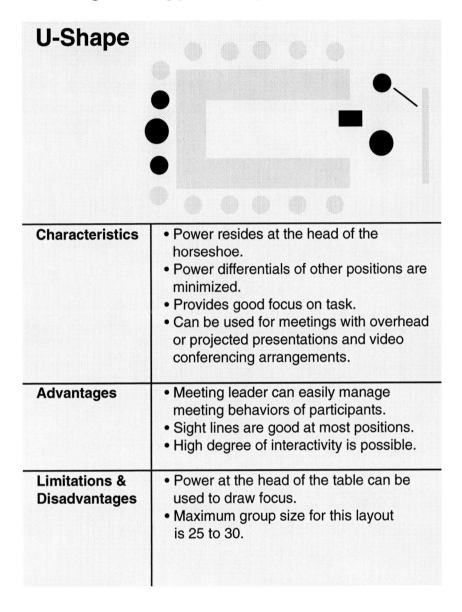

3

Characteristics	• Power resides at the head of the horseshoe. • Power differentials of other positions are minimized. • Provides good focus on task. • Can be used for meetings with overhead or projected presentations and video conferencing arrangements.
Advantages	• Meeting leader can easily manage meeting behaviors of participants. • Sight lines are good at most positions. • High degree of interactivity is possible.
Limitations & Disadvantages	• Power at the head of the table can be used to draw focus. • Maximum group size for this layout is 25 to 30.

Semi-Circle (without table)

Characteristics	• Power resides in the center of the semi-circle. • Power differentials of other positions are minimized. • Provides good focus on task.
Advantages	• Meeting leader can easily manage meeting behaviors of participants. • Sight lines are good at all positions. • High degree of interactivity is possible.
Limitations & Disadvantages	• Not good for meetings with overhead or projected presentations, or with extensive paper materials. • No place for coffee cups or juice glasses; note-taking must be done on laps. • Maximum group size for this layout is 10 to 15.

Oval and Rectangle

Characteristics	• Power resides at the head and foot of the table or at the center of one side, depending on where the ranking participant sits. • Power differentials are substantial. • Provides close interaction.
Advantages	• Sight lines are good at most positions. • High degree of interactivity is possible. • Adequate table space available.
Limitations & Disadvantages	• Not good for meetings with overhead or projected presentations. • Maximum manageable group size for this layout is 15 to 20.

3

Truncated Oval with Presenter and Recorder

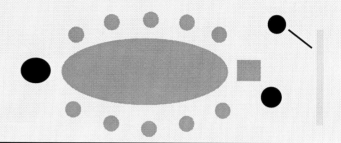

Characteristics	• Power resides at the head at the presenter position. • Power differentials of other positions are minimized. • Provides good focus on task. • Can be used for meetings with overhead or projected presentations.
Advantages	• Meeting leader can easily manage meeting behaviors of participants. • Sight lines are good at most positions. • High degree of interactivity is possible.
Limitations & Disadvantages	• Power at the head of the table can be used to draw focus from the front of the room and the presenter. • Not suitable for video conferencing arrangements. • Maximum group size for this layout is 10 to15.

U-Shape with Side Seating

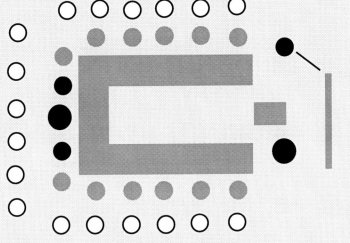

3

Characteristics	• Power resides at the head and in the center of the horseshoe. • Power differentials are minimized among other positions at the main table. • Provides good focus on task • Can be used for meetings with projected presentations.
Advantages	• Meeting leader can manage behaviors of participants at the main table and monitor rear and side seating. • Sight lines are good for most at the main table, but visibility from the head position to the rear seating is awkward. • High degree of interactivity is possible.
Limitations & Disadvantages	• Power at the head of the table can be used to draw focus from the front of the room and the presenter. • Maximum group size for this layout is 40 to 50.

Classroom

Characteristics	• Classic layout for informational presentations and training. • Power resides at the front of the room, but differentials among other participants are minimal. • Projected presentations are best, especially in larger rooms. • Some capability for interaction via Q&A.
Advantages	• Meeting leader can manage some behaviors of participants. • Forward-looking sight lines are good at most positions. • Table space is available for coffee, juice, papers and other meeting materials.
Limitations & Disadvantages	• Not suitable for video conferencing arrangements. • Limited interaction capability among participants. • Susceptible to inattention and side conversations. • Without unusual preparations, 50 to 60 is typically the maximum group size.

Round Table

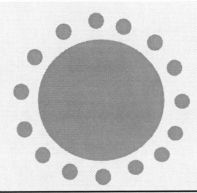

Characteristics	• Power resides where the ranking participant sits. • Power differentials among other seating positions are not substantial. • This layout provides for close and potentially intense interaction.
Advantages	• Sight lines are good at all positions. • Adequate space for coffee cups and juice glasses. Note-taking and paper handouts are not a problem.
Limitations & Disadvantages	• Not good for meetings with overhead or projected presentations. • Use of flip charts to record is limited. • Because a high degree of interactivity is possible, it brings with it the risk of higher levels of open conflict. • Group size for this layout is limited by the table; typically 12 to 24 max.

3

Circle (without table)

Characteristics	• Power resides where the ranking participant sits. • Power differentials among other seating positions are small. • Interaction will be close, and possibly intense.
Advantages	• Sight lines are good at all positions. • Encourages participation, directness, and candor. • Highly flexible—quick transitions to break-out groups or stand-up exercises.
Limitations & Disadvantages	• No space for coffee cups and juice glasses; writing must be done on participants laps. • Not suitable for meetings with projected presentations. • Use of flip charts to record for the total group is limited. • Group size for this layout is limited to 25 to 40 by need for eye contact.

Restaurants and Cafeterias

Characteristics	• The person who buys lunch also buys implicit power, but may not hold the upper hand depending on existing relationships among the participants. • Power differentials are substantial, but not based on seating position. • Provides close interaction.
Advantages	• Sight lines are good at most positions. • High degree of interactivity is possible; informal setting can support relationship building.
Limitations & Disadvantages	• Not a good setting for private or sensitive matters. • Can be noisy and fraught with interruptions. • Not suitable for meetings requiring overhead or projected presentations. • Not compatible with formal facilitation. • Max manageable group size for this layout is 4 to 6.

3

Small Theater Set-Up for Hotel Meeting Rooms

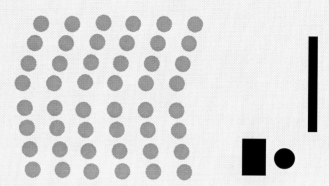

Characteristics
- Classic layout for larger informational presentations.
- Power clearly resides at the front of the room.
- Projected presentations are usually required.
- Some capability for interaction and feedback to the presenter via Q & A if roving microphones are used.

Advantages
- Facilitator or meeting leader can manage some meeting behaviors of participants, (for example, by choosing who to call on in Q & A), and controls the group via the power of the front of the room.
- With proper planning, forward looking sight lines are good at most positions—participants can see the presenter and the presentation screen.

Limitations &
- Not suitable for video conferencing arrangements, unless the camera focuses solely on the presenter.
- Flip charts don't work well for group memory.
- No space for coffee, and juice, papers and other meeting materials.
- Limited interaction capability among participants.
- Susceptible to negative behaviors by attendees such as inattention and side conversations.
- Need to use ushers or block back rows to assure filling the front rows first.
- Maximum group size for this layout is largely dependent on room size, type of projection and screen size. With a single screen of ordinary size, the upper limit for this layout is 75-80.

Self-Check: Chapter Three Review

Answers to the following questions appear on page 102.

1. List four factors that you should consider when determining your meeting room layout.

   1. _____

   2. _____

   3. _____

   4. _____

3

2. Which of the following arrangements provides the greatest power differential?
   a. U-shape
   b. Oval or rectangle
   c. Round table

3. Which of the following arrangements allows for the greatest number of people?
   a. Semi-circle without table
   b. Truncated oval with presenter and recorder
   c. Small theater

4. Which of the following arrangements allows for effective use of overhead or projected presentations?
   a. Classroom
   b. Round table
   c. Oval or rectangle

5. Which of the following arrangements gives the facilitator least control over participant meeting behavior?
   a. U-shape
   b. Semi-circle without table
   c. Theater seating

Chapter *Four*

Advanced Methods

Chapter Objectives

▶ Follow a logical sequencing of meeting elements.

▶ Explain stakeholder analysis and political mapping methods.

▶ Prepare for important meetings using the **Three-Dimensional Outline**™.

This chapter looks in depth at some of the key meeting preparation tasks and suggests advanced methods for your consideration. If you're new to meeting management, you may want to skip ahead to Chapter Five to get the full picture of the meeting management process, and come back to this when you're ready for more details.

For meeting leaders who already have the basics in hand, this chapter can provide some high-leverage techniques for building agendas, selecting participants, and preparing for very critical meetings.

Develop a Logical Sequence for Your Meeting

Decide how your going to sequence your material.

Take a look at everything you have in front of you. By now, you have an idea of who your participants will be, and you've completed your objectives and defined your desired outcomes. You have selected a meeting facility, drafted your agenda, and gotten an idea of what topics will and won't be in scope for this session. Now, you need to decide on how you're going to sequence the material.

The sequences below are some of the most common arrangements for organizing material. You can use one or mix and match them to suit the specific task at hand.

Sequencing Method	Description	Characteristics and Tips
Past to present	Presents material chronologically	Works well when you need to cover historical periods or trace the development of a product, position, or concept.
Priority	Presents material in order of its relative importance.	Particularly useful for those times when you have a lot to cover and are likely to run out of time before you finish the topics to be discussed.
Advantages and Disadvantages	Presents a point in such a way to show its up side and down side.	This is especially good for presenting controversial material or making a one-way presentation of information to a group before a decision is made.
Pain to pleasure	Moves the group through a review of an unfortunate but correctable situation in order to drive towards possible solutions.	Approach is useful when not all stakeholders agree that there is a problem, or when an urgent call to action is needed.
Categorical	Requires the creation of categories for your material. You might organize your material into sections such as "Features and Benefits", "Competitive Comparisons," or "Heroes and Villains."	1. The categorical arrangement is good when you are dealing with complex topics 2. For longer meetings, allows people to come for selected segments where they have specific contributions.

● Advanced Methods

Sequencing Method	Description	Characteristics and Tips
Functional	Divides discussion of an issue into segments based on functional views, such as Finance, Marketing, Manufacturing, Human Resources, etc.	1. Very useful for framing issues where involvement is required from several parts of the organization. 2. As with the categorical approach, it may allow subject matter experts to arrive for their piece and leave.
Geographic/ Regional	Divides discussion of an issue into segments based on regional considerations, such as North America, Europe, Asia-Pacific, etc.	This approach is good at pulling out considerations on an issue that may vary based on cultural or market differences, around the country or around the globe.
Mixed	Uses different sequencing methods for various segments of longer meetings. For example, your introduction might employ Past to Present; then your initial segment might use a Priority sequence, and your closing might summarize actions on a regional or functional basis.	1. Use the correct tool for the job at hand. 2. Well-defined desired outcomes will provide good clues as to which sequence might be best. 3. Experiment with these arrangements, and especially in longer sessions, use variety to keep the group alive and engaged. Your participants will appreciate it.

Take a Moment

Thinking back on the last meeting you attended, what sequencing method was used? Was it effective for the desired outcomes involved in that sessions? Record your thoughts below:

Sequencing Method: _____

Effectiveness: _____

_____

_____

_____

_____

4

Performing a Stakeholder Analysis

Determining whom your participants will be is a potentially critical step in preparing for a meeting, and a very common source of failures. This section contains our thoughts on how to approach the *who* question.

As with other decisions the meeting planner needs to make, there are several alternative ways of looking at the participant question. The table below identifies some of the more common logic flows. In fact, you'll probably want to try several approaches before making your final selections, and then repeat the process when you check the availability of key people.

There are several alternative ways of looking at the participant question.

● Advanced Methods

Participant Selection Method	Description	Characteristics and Tips
Functional	Ensures representation from stakeholders in all affected functional such as Finance, areas, Marketing, Manufacturing, Human Resources, etc.	Useful for framing issues where involvement is required from several parts of the organization.
Geographic/ Regional	Determines participation based on regional considerations, such as North America, Europe, Asia-Pacific, etc.	This approach is good for discussion of matters that may vary based on cultural or market differences around the country or around the globe.
Key Staffs	Identifies peripheral groups that may have equity in the direction established in the meeting or may have work to do as a result of decisions made by others, such as Public Affairs, Legal Counsel, Finance, Shareholder Relations, etc.	Failure to keep key groups in the loop can cause rework, or diminish the effectiveness of otherwise well thought out plans.
Level	Determines the rank of participants involved, often as an overlay to other methods.	• Don't invite the global marketing vice president if the sales manager for the Chicago Region can make the decision. • Conversely, don't expect the local HR associate to change the compensation plans for the organization.

Participant Selection Method	Description	Characteristics and Tips
Max-Mix	Seeks to involve a broad array of diverse viewpoints, such as people from different disciplines, different levels, different geographic localities, etc.	• Excellent for brainstorming solutions to knotty issues. • Must leave rank at the door to ensure participation of lower level people.
Pain Absorbers (Pleasure Seekers)	Includes primarily the people who are on the front line of an issue and can describe an opportunity or challenge in great detail.	Approach is useful when there is awareness of an issue but it isn't well defined.
Political Mapping	Determines in advance of the meeting who has power on a particular issue and what their going in position is or might be. Typically used as an overlay to other methods. A sample worksheet is shown later in this section	Very important tool to determine who NOT to invite to meetings (those with little power to influence decisions but with strongly opposing views).
Subject Matter Expertise	Identifies subject matter experts (SMEs) who have in-depth knowledge on a particular topic. Usually an overlay to other selection methods used to assure that factual information needed by decision-makers is readily available.	Good facilitation is necessary to ensure that the SME is heard but doesn't bog the group down in levels of detail not required to achieve the desired outcomes.

Participant Selection Method	Description	Characteristics and Tips
Supporters and Opponents	Involves people from both sides of an issue and ensures that discussion will show both up side and down side views.	• This is especially good for discussing controversial material if you want to assure that all views are put on the table. • Sometimes you need to do two meetings, one including only supporters and another with opponents, followed by a politically-mapped meeting with decision-makers.

Take a Moment

Think ahead to the next meeting you will be conducting. What participant selection techniques might you use?

❑ Functional

❑ Geographic/Regional

❑ Key Staffs

❑ Level

❑ Max-Mix

❑ Pain Absorbers (Pleasure Seekers)

❑ Political Mapping

❑ Subject Matter Expertise

❑ Supporters and Opponents

Creating a Political Map Worksheet

Another way to lay out key stakeholders involves considering their potential influence on a decision or direction and their existing position on the matter. This approach is particularly useful when you are dealing with highly controversial issues and need to anticipate specific positions or concerns in advance of the meeting.

There are no hard and fast rules on whom to invite; the point is to think about whom you need on board to resolve the topic at hand and what influence various individuals may have both on the content of the discussion and on group dynamics. Take a look at the form on the next page and think about how you might use it.

4

Political Map Worksheet

Issue:

Desired Outcome:

Individual Name	Power to Influence Outcome	Strength of Position on Issue (known or assumed)	Key elements of view or position	Invite?
	1 2 3 4 5 low high	-5 -4 -3 -2 -1 Neutral +1 +2 +3 +4 +5		Yes No
	1 2 3 4 5 low high	-5 -4 -3 -2 -1 Neutral +1 +2 +3 +4 +5		Yes No
	1 2 3 4 5 low high	-5 -4 -3 -2 -1 Neutral +1 +2 +3 +4 +5		Yes No
	1 2 3 4 5 low high	-5 -4 -3 -2 -1 Neutral +1 +2 +3 +4 +5		Yes No
	1 2 3 4 5 low high	-5 -4 -3 -2 -1 Neutral +1 +2 +3 +4 +5		Yes No
	1 2 3 4 5 low high	-5 -4 -3 -2 -1 Neutral +1 +2 +3 +4 +5		Yes No
	1 2 3 4 5 low high	-5 -4 -3 -2 -1 Neutral +1 +2 +3 +4 +5		Yes No
	1 2 3 4 5 low high	-5 -4 -3 -2 -1 Neutral +1 +2 +3 +4 +5		Yes No
	1 2 3 4 5 low high	-5 -4 -3 -2 -1 Neutral +1 +2 +3 +4 +5		Yes No

Important Note:

Political maps, because they tend to use brief (and perhaps blunt) statements about issues and positions that are based largely on opinions, should be treated as very sensitive documents. Generally, they are intended for the personal and private use of the meeting leader and should not be circulated.

Preparing for Important Meetings

Some meetings deserve more preparation than usual—those one-time opportunities or challenges where major progress can occur if everything goes just right. In these cases, the experienced meeting leader will double, triple, or quadruple the normal preparation time and effort to maximize the probability of success. Here's a template for an intense preparation plan.

Some meetings deserve more preparation than usual.

Step 1

Gather your notes, starting with the desired outcomes you've defined and the tentative agenda in which you've identified topic(s) to be covered and planned your sequencing method. Have your political map handy and a sketch of the room layout you plan to use.

Step 2

Interrogate yourself on the situation using the reporter's questions in order to identify limitations and opportunities. The following is a list of thought-starters, but it is not exhaustive. Build your own list tailored to the situation at hand.

Reporter's Question Type	Typical Questions
What?	1. What are we trying to do, both in the meeting and as a result of the meeting? (This should tie directly to your desired outcomes). 2. What will success look like? 3. What can go wrong that would ruin the meeting? 4. What prework or prereading have participants done? 5. What could someone say that would trigger positive outcomes? 6. What might someone say that would undermine progress? 7. What known roadblocks need to be overcome?

continued on the next page

4

Reporter's Question Type	Typical Questions
	8. What natural support is present? 9. What questions will participants ask? 10. What facts or data should be available?
When?	1. When is the meeting? 2. Is this the best time? (What is going on immediately before and after session that could influence the disposition or outlook of key participants?)
Why?	1. Why would each participant want to support what I hope the meeting will accomplish? 2. Why would specific participants want to derail my plan?
How?	1. How can I emphasize the positives? 2. How, and in what order, should I present the plan? 3. How can I demonstrate that all contingencies have been provided for?
How much?	1. How much time do we have for the meeting? 2. How much time do we have to prepare for the meeting? 3. How much money are we taking about? 4. Do we have the budget?

continued on the next page

Reporter's Question Type	Typical Questions
How long?	1. How long do attendees have to make a decision on the meeting topic? 2. How long before we have to have a plan in place? 3. How long do we expect it to take before the plan has impact?
Where?	1. Where are we meeting? 2. Does the meeting room layout support the degree and type of interaction needed to achieve the desired outcomes and make the players comfortable?
Follow-up	Many of the above can be answered positively or negatively. For those that don't come out strongly positive, ask follow-up questions, such as: 1. If not, why not? 2. If not here, then where? 3. If not now, then when? 4. If not these people, then who? 5. If not this much, how much can we afford? Follow this process of questioning until you arrive at answers that minimize risk and maximize opportunities for success.

4

Step 3

Summarize what you've learned using the **Three-Dimensional Outline™** illustrated on page 57. In this context, the 3-D helps you refine your agenda, consider the sequence of topics, and review the make-it or break-it steps you need to accomplish to reach your goals for the session.

A Three-Dimensional Outline™ is like an agenda within an agenda.

◆ In some respects, it can be considered an agenda within an agenda, but for the meeting planners eyes only. You need to be direct and candid with yourself, but you need not disclose everything to your participants via the published agenda.

◆ Many agenda builders tend to focus only on the *what* questions, and disregard the very important dimensions of *why* and *how*.

  • *Why* questions are important for meeting your desired outcomes (especially in the context of the specific participants you are working with and their initial positions).

  • *How* questions sensitize you to the materials and equipment you may need to bring home the key points, and also may suggest the need for rehearsals and/or collaboration with key participants in advance of the meeting.

This simple matrix will expand quickly as you consider the answers to questions in your self-interrogation above. An easy way to approach this is to put it in table form on your computer so you can add categories readily. Landscape format is best so you have plenty of room on the right to answer the why questions. The left-hand columns should be direct lifts from your draft agenda—when you are done with your analysis, you can export them back to your final agenda.

Take a Moment

Go through the sample **Three-Dimensional Outline™** on page 57. Pay special attention to the *how* and *why* columns to look for techniques that you may want to use more frequently and for rationale for use of the various techniques illustrated.

Three-Dimensional Outline™ for Meeting Preparation

Set-Up Categories	Questions	Why?
Facility	Right room, right size, right equipment, assigned seating?	
People	Right people coming?	
Date, Time & Duration	Right time, enough time?	
Equipment & Props	On hand & functional?	

Time	What Topic and Desired Outcomes	Who	How	Why? (& Notes for special emphasis)
:05	Introductions Make sure everyone knows each other and what activity they are from.	Leader (Chris) and Group	Round-the-table self introductions.	• Remember to reinforce Jane as SME on HR matters • Make it clear that Sue is the major stakeholder with budget approval authority and that Pete will be implementing whatever the group develops
:10	Background Make sure the group understands the situation in detail to be ready to develop actions.	Bill (SME)	Chronological review of how the situation has developed and need for action.	• Caution the group to focus on what has happened and what needs to be done versus "who dunnit".
:10	Solution Development (generate ideas).	Chris and Group	Brainstorm	• Remember to go through rules for brainstorming.
:10	Solution Development (review ideas and rank.)	Chris and Group	Combine and rank best ideas.	*continued on the next page*

Time	What Topic and Desired Outcomes	Who	How	Why? (& Notes for special emphasis)
:10	Solution Development (validate practicality and estimate costs).	Chris and Group	Evaluate— Assess each element for cost and feasibility.	• Remind group that we are spending Sue's money and that Pete has to implement. • Verify that Jane is comfortable with plan.
:05	Agree on solution.	Chris and Group	Agree, and determine who does what by when.	• Carefully document agreement and plans & commitments for next steps.
:05	Recap and evaluate meeting	Chris and Group	Recap agreements and next steps. Use round-robin callouts to evaluate meeting.	• Thank Sally for flying in. • Acknowledge Jane's work (ahead of the meeting) that made a productive meeting possible. • Thank Sue for stepping up to fund the solution, and thank Pete in advance for making it happen.

Self-Check: Chapter Four Review

In the space below, identify one benefit for each of the methods discussed in the chapter. Answers appear on page 103.

Advanced Method	Benefit

1. Choosing logical sequences for your meeting.   _____

2. Using the Stakeholder Analysis method for participant selection   _____

3. Using Political Mapping   _____

4

4. Using the **Three Dimensional Outline**™ for Meeting Preparation   _____

Chapter *Five*

Meetings as a Performing Art

Chapter Objectives

▶ Understand the *going on-stage* mindset.

▶ Create favorable first impressions.

▶ Recognize key roles.

▶ Understand the central role of the facilitator.

▶ Explain the importance of evaluations.

▶ How to move from agreement to action through documented agreements and work plans.

Getting Ready to Go on Stage

Meetings are a showcase for and a test of communication and leadership skills.

Meetings are a showcase for and a test of communication and leadership skills. Meeting leaders and facilitators must mentally prepare for each session as if they were going on-stage. The best meetings have someone at the front of the room who is:

◆ Skilled in group dynamics.

◆ Clearly in charge of the process.

◆ Familiar with the desired outcomes.

Conducting the Meeting

The Best Surprise Is No Surprise

Someone should arrive early to confirm readiness of facility, materials, and equipment. Early arrival is especially important for larger meetings and when using outside facilities such as hotels.

Opening the Session—First Impressions

At the beginning of the meeting, the Leader or Facilitator should welcome participants, introduce newcomers and guests, thank hosts or sponsors, and generally set the tone for the meeting.

Scoping the Work—Goals and Agenda

Before diving into the work, answer the "Why are we here?" question for participants by clarifying the purpose and desired outcomes for the meeting. Then quickly preview the agenda to answer other key questions, including "*How* are we going to go about this?" and "About *how long* will it take?"

Next discuss and agree on ground rules to define "*How* should we behave?" and "*What* should we expect?" This includes housekeeping items such as:

◆ Timing of breaks and meals.

◆ Location of restrooms, telephones, and smoking areas.

Ground rules also include meeting process matters such as:

◆ Guidelines on participation and Q&A.

◆ Guidelines on time extensions, content changes, digressions, and off-subject discussions.

Identify Key Roles—"Who Is Supposed to Do What?"

Establishing roles can be very important, especially in sessions involving people that don't normally work together or in meetings with aggressive goals and tight time constraints. Here are some key meeting roles:

◆ **Meeting or Segment Leader**—Drives for achievement of desired outcome for the meeting or a segment of it. May also be subject matter expert or central stakeholder.

◆ **Presenter**—Front-of-room person who presents material; may be subject matter expert or representative of a particular constituency. Can be easily combined with segment leader role.

> **Before diving into the work, answer the "Why are we here?" question for participants.**

5

61

♦ **Facilitator**—Drives to achieve process goals—timeliness, efficiency, full participation, maximum buy-in, etc. Can be combined with meeting leader in some circumstances, but objectivity or focus may suffer.

♦ **Recorder**—In charge of note taking and documentation for post-meeting purposes. (meeting/segment leaders and facilitators should generally not serve as recorders due to the lack of objectivity.)

♦ **Timekeeper**—Provides the facilitator and meeting/segment leaders with information about time remaining.

♦ **Participant**—Listens actively and contributes at appropriate times.

Important Note

In smaller or less formal sessions, the distinct roles identified above often are combined, with one person doing more than one thing.

When this is the case, all need to recognize that some functionality will be compromised, and participants should be encouraged to help fill gaps and observe when, for example, the Leader/Facilitator needs help in maintaining objectivity.

Take a Moment

Reflect for a moment on the value of assigning key roles. From your perspective, identify two critical functions for meeting leadership.

1. _____

2. _____

Moving Through the Agenda

With your purpose and desired outcomes defined, and your ground rules and roles set, you're ready to get to work. As you lead the group through the agenda, here are the functions you will provide as a skilled leader or facilitator.

Guide Participants

Think of yourself as a guide leading people through the meeting process with sensitivity to both the desired outcomes and the needs of the individuals involved. You will need to:

♦ Maintain time and subject matter discipline by starting on time, sticking to the subject, and ending on time.

♦ Select the appropriate level of control for the group and the task, noting that strong facilitation may be needed for certain groups and/or controversial subject matter; both prevention and intervention may be used to avoid or manage conflict.

A need for changes in pacing or approach may occur during the meeting. The skilled facilitator is flexible and does not stick to the rules for the rules' sake.

5

> Think of yourself as a guide, leading people through the meeting process.

Involve Everyone

The person at the front of the room must ensure broad involvement and candid participation by all. Send the "OK to talk" message early to draw out the reticent, and constantly monitor interactions to avoid these common problems:

◆ Domination of discussion by a few.

◆ Side conversations and inattention.

◆ Redundant presentation—If prereading materials were provided, be sure that presenters do not reread the entire texts to the participants unless it is very clear that the majority did not do their homework.

◆ Language issues, including lexicon and acronym use—Make sure all know the meaning of acronyms and agree on the meaning of words. Much confusion and disagreement can be created by these simple-to-correct problems.

◆ Dodging (avoidance of responsibility).

◆ Digression/Lack of focus.

◆ Unwillingness to commit/Trouble reaching agreement.

Use the Best Tools

Skilled meeting leaders use a full range of meeting tools—the familiar "brainstorming" technique is just one of many. Try some of these:

◆ Breakout groups for problem solving.

◆ Fishbone diagrams for expansion of issues.

◆ Prioritizing to determine sequence of actions.

◆ Plus/minus lists to evaluate alternatives, etc.

Interact with People in Important Supporting Roles

Regularly check in with team members who can help you move the meeting along. The timekeeper provides important support. He or she must pay attention to the clock and provide timing information to the facilitator, segment leader, and presenter. In turn, the person at the front of the room must keep an eye on the timekeeper and acknowledge signals the timekeeper provides. For the timekeeper to be effective, a timed agenda with good estimates of time requirements for each segment is needed.

The recorder also supports the facilitator and meeting/segment leaders and takes direction from them:

◆ The Recorder should take notes on agreements, assignments, and timing (in a level of detail appropriate to the subject matter) and capture other items for group memory as required.

◆ In fast-paced brainstorming sessions, two or more recorders may be necessary to avoid slowing the group.

◆ The best recorders are those with some familiarity with the subject matter and vocabulary but who are not participants/not actively involved in the matter at hand.

5

Confirm Agreements and Assignments

To translate meeting agreements into action, confirm and document all assignments before closing the meeting. In lengthy or complicated sessions, recap at the end of each topic and then summarize at the end of the meeting.

Confirm and document all assignments before closing the meeting.

Documentation of agreements and commitments is key to ensuring that people will follow through and do what they are supposed to do. The use of a *Meeting Agreements and Assignments* flip chart or projected computer image during a meeting is the best way to be sure that your agreements have clarity and buy-in.

Evaluate the Session

Before closing, evaluate the session formally or informally. Evaluations are important and provide multiple benefits—most meetings need formal evaluation to:

◆ Provide an opportunity for participants to give feedback to meeting organizers (positive and negative), bring closure to the event, and help consolidate buy-in to outcomes of the session.

◆ Capture and convey valuable information to meeting organizers relative to the quality of the results, the satisfaction level of the participants, and clues on how future sessions can be improved.

Evaluations can be done easily. Using a device as simple as a +/- list, and/or a numerical scoring system, a meeting can be evaluated in five minutes or less. Interactive methods that gain more information take somewhat longer, depending on group size.

Leave enough time for evaluation.

Because the evaluation is the last item on the agenda, meeting leaders need to be sure to leave enough time for it.

◆ Evaluation inputs will be better if the instrument is provided at the beginning of the meeting or well before adjournment.

◆ Some participants will view a skipped evaluation as an attempt on the part of the facilitator to avoid a negative rating.

When asking participants for live feedback, the facilitator should lead the effort and solicit information relative to the following:

◆ **Results**—The extent to which desired outcomes were achieved.

◆ **Process**—The quality of actions that led to the results (participation, candor, timeliness, etc.).

◆ **Overall satisfaction** of participants.

Adjourn the session

Signaling a clear end to the meeting is important. Participants (especially junior people) need to know that it's alright to leave even though some post-meeting conversations may take place.

Following Up

Attention to work done after the meeting can dramatically improve results. Consider these points during your follow-up efforts.

Use Documentation in Follow-Up

When agreements are well documented during the meeting, follow-up efforts to are greatly simplified. Here are a few common techniques that can be very effective:

◆ Publish minutes or notes within 24 hours of the meeting. Put agreements and assignments near the top of the document and highlight names of people responsible and the due dates.

> **Publish minutes or notes within 24 hours of the meeting.**

◆ For larger or more complex projects, translate meeting agreements and assignments into a timed work plan. Publish this within a few days and the meeting and ask assignees to validate the translation and provide status comments at appropriate intervals.

5

◆ For items that may had questionable buy-in (e.g. "I'll *try* to get that report before next time"), make a personal contact with the individual involved to solidify the commitment. If the item is really important and the person is short of time or resources, you may need to support the individual with a formal request to management.

◆ Publish the agenda for the next session well in advance and highlight key open assignments and names of responsible individuals in the cover note. For those that you suspect may be struggling, call a few days in advance to reinforce the importance of the assignment and reconfirm their ability to deliver.

Good documentation also facilitates the implementation of action plans and permits easy communication of information to persons not in attendance. Well-written action plans are easily relayed to those not in attendance to generate prompt response to direction established in the meeting. Additionally, these action plans allow updates to stakeholders not present on a routine basis.

Self-Check: Chapter Five Review

Answers to the following questions appear on pages 103 and 104.

	True	False
1. A good meeting leader can conduct an excellent meeting without understanding the desired outcomes.	_____	_____
2. You can save time at the outset of the meeting by getting directly to the task.	_____	_____
3. Role assignments aren't important when the leader is the facilitator and recorder.	_____	_____
4. Though consistency is important; skilled facilitators will change pacing or approach when the situation warrants.	_____	_____
5. Involvement of all isn't important as long as you get to the answer you're seeking.	_____	_____
6. Evaluations should focus clearly on the results of the session.	_____	_____
7. Timekeepers should interrupt presenters if they have run over their allotted time.	_____	_____

	True	False

8. The preferred form of follow-up documentation is the timed work plan.   _____   _____

9. Informal documentation is OK when the need for buy-in by nonparticipants is low.   _____   _____

5

Chapter *Six*

What If Something Goes Wrong?

Chapter Objectives

▶ Effectively manage the "spread the heat" meeting.

▶ Revitalize meetings that have gone from routine to rut.

▶ Avoid domination and achieve broad participation.

▶ Deal with possible distractions from the agenda.

"**W**hen the boss herded us into the conference room at 4:30 and slammed the door, it was clear something BIG was bothering him, and we weren't there to discuss the menu for the company picnic," Chris recalled. "Even though I normally chair the staff meetings, I hadn't ever seen him this angry, and didn't know what I could do to help. So, I just sat there and let it unroll, not sure of what to do next."

Even in organizations that value effective meeting management, meetings can go awry.

Even in organizations that value effective meeting management, meetings can go awry. Managers can lose their cool, team members can clam up just when you need their input, and normally good team players can forget to do what they said they would do. Sometimes there aren't perfect solutions to problems like these, but the skilled meeting leader can be equipped with a prompt and correct response to help cut losses. Following are suggestions on how to deal with some of the substantive challenges meeting leaders can face.

Handling a "Spread the Heat" Meeting

Organization or department heads can become uncharacteristically emotional when faced with a crisis, such as unexpectedly low profits, an unfavorable press review, an incident with an important customer, or failure on the part of a key supplier.

Because the news is unexpected, a typical reaction is to "round up the usual suspects" and spread the grief, with little or no planning regarding desired outcomes, appropriate attendees, or anything else. So what do you do as the voice of reason and the champion of meeting management?

◆ First, *don't* say "calm down, boss," as this is likely to have the opposite result. Second, go with the flow and let him or her vent. Provide confirming comments as required to demonstrate your support for the seriousness of the concern and passion for a timely solution, but don't join the feeding frenzy if fingers are being pointed.

◆ When the chief has finished with the description of the issue, offer to recap the situation using the reporter's questions to ensure that all understand the details of the situation and to begin an action plan. In this offer, you'll likely need to move attention away from "*Who* did it?" to "*What* do we need to do now?"

◆ Once you've recapped the situation, suggest a pause to be sure that the right people are in the room to proceed with development of solutions. This can be as simple as a question to the group along the lines of "do we have the right people here to solve this?"

◆ If the answer is no, you may want to summon others, if they are available, or partition the work so that some actions can be initiated immediately with more to follow when appropriate people can be reached.

◆ Even if all necessary people are available, it may be appropriate to suggest an overnight delay to permit organization of a follow-up session with clearly defined desired outcomes and some preparation on the part of participants.

◆ If the urgency of the situation (or the patience of the boss) does not permit an overnight delay, even a short break can be appropriate. This can allow reconvening with clearer thinking, the right information and materials, and at least a rudimentary agenda.

When the chief has finished with the description of the issue, offer to recap the situation using the reporter's questions

6

If you are normally your team's the meeting leader, it is your responsibility to help the boss refocus from "*What* happened?" to "*What* is our plan to recover from this?" These situations provide a good showcase for your ability to lead the group toward positive results. If there isn't a designated meeting leader, these situations provide a great opportunity for anyone in the group to take an ad-hoc leadership role and help the team work through the issue.

Take a Moment

Go through the scenario above and find issues that you've faced before, and perhaps did not anticipate fully. In the space below, note actions that you may want to consider in the future to react more positively and effectively.

_____

_____

_____

_____

Breaking Out of Ruts

"Routine" can turn into "rut" with groups that meet on a regular basis.

"Routine" can turn into "rut" with groups that meet on a regular basis. "The same old stuff" is a major limiting factor for staff meetings, standing committees, and others that meet on a recurring basis.

The meeting always begins with the budget report and we're always in need of a little more funding. Fred always arrives 10 minutes late with a bad excuse. Sally usually leaves early, for an "important appointment." Pat brings his mail and discusses it with Chris. Over the months that the group has been meeting, substantive (or potentially controversial) issues have disappeared from the agenda, and many participants feel as if they are going through the motions instead of using their time productively.

If you're the chair of the group, you can take action at once when you recognize the symptoms. If you're not the chair, you can still help by contacting the meeting organizer privately and suggesting actions to revitalize the group. Either way, there are things you can do to inject energy by upseting the status quo. Shake things up by:

> **Inject energy by upseting the status quo.**

◆ **Changing the setting and the layout.**
You've been meeting in the Executive Conference Room around an oval table. Move to conference room 202 and set the room up in a horseshoe. Provide place cards to assign seating.

◆ **Changing the content or mode of presentations.**
If you've been using printed handouts during your meetings, ask presenters to create a projected presentation instead of distributing paper; if you're using projected presentations, switch to one-page papers or flip charts. Change presentations from "status reports" to "issues only" material.

◆ **Changing the time and/or duration.**
Your standing time was 8:00 to 10:00 a.m. on Tuesdays. Take a sharp pencil to the agenda and make it one hour, beginning at 8:30 a.m. on Monday.

6

◆ **Reversing and revising the agenda.**
Put Fred on first, and ask that he do a 10-minute summary of issues from his area that are of interest to the entire group for the next meeting. Put Sally on last, and ask that she bring in a synopsis of a different customer issue for each of the next few meetings.

◆ **Bringing in an outside speaker.**
Suppliers, dealers, customers, employees and other people outside your team almost always have diverse views on the challenges and opportunities your organization faces. Bring them in to deliver the message in person.

◆ **Adding food and/or music.**
Something as simple as having coffee and bagels, if you haven't been doing it, can help renew your group. Consider kicking-off a new month, new year, or special promotion by having the top ranking members of your group serve

breakfast (caterers can bring it, but put the leaders in aprons to do the serving). For this kind of event, you can also add music—recorded or live.

◆ **Taking a tour.**
Combine your meeting with a visit to someone else's facility—a plant, a customer site, a supplier, etc. Borrow a conference room and do an agenda that tailors your topics to the view from that location.

◆ **Do a stand-up meeting.**
Shorten the agenda, and have the meeting in the cafeteria or lobby without chairs. Bring enough flip charts on easels to allow one for every three or four group members. Use the charts to support a breakout group exercise to brainstorm ways to revitalize the group.

◆ **Bring in a facilitator and recharter the group.**
Using an objective outsider, revisit the purpose of the group and develop a new charter document. You may decide you don't need the meeting at all (yeah!), or you may find that you truly need to refocus on issues that the group hasn't been addressing.

Putting up with the "same old stuff" in recurring meetings isn't acceptable for either meeting leaders or participants. If you're not happy with the outcomes or efficiency of the meetings you attend, find a way to do something about it.

Take a Moment

Think about the recurring meetings that you attend, and assess them as to their effectiveness. If your meetings are less than satisfactory, what can you do to precipitate a change for the better? If your meetings are OK for now, what will you do to avoid slipping into a rut?

_____

_____

_____

Achieving Broad Participation

Achieving a high degree of participating and involvement is one of the biggest challenges a Meeting Leader or Facilitator faces. Meetings involving considerable diversity among the participants escalate the degree of difficulty on this front, but also offer the potential to yield really creative solutions when the facilitator is effective. Of course, prevention is the best measure—setting ground rules that encourage participation, sending "OK to talk" messages early in the session, and so on.

But what if your set-up wasn't totally effective, and you need to increase involvement during the meeting?

◆ What do you do if someone isn't participating in the meeting? How can you get that person to give input?

◆ What if someone tries to take over the meeting and won't let others give their ideas?

The first step toward solutions for these issues is recognition that there is a problem. While it's obvious to the person who is not being heard, it isn't always clear to the person at the front of the room or the head of the table. If the person who is talking a lot has a plausible solution, it may not be viewed as domination by those who agree with the line of thought. Constant monitoring by the Meeting Leader or Facilitator is needed to be sure that subtle domination or lack of comments from others is not limiting participation. Here are some ways you can assess participation during the meeting:

◆ **Monitor "talk time" and ask questions.**
Without being obvious, make mental or brief written notes to indicate who has provided comments on a particular topic before closing it out. For those who have not said anything, you can say things like:

• "Before we move on, do you have anything to add to this—Pete? Jane?"

• "How does this look from the HR perspective, John?"

• "Well, group, does anyone have anything else on their mind that we ought to consider here?"

> Achieving a high degree of participating and involvement is one of the biggest challenges a Meeting Leader or Facilitator faces.

6

● What If Something Goes Wrong?

◆ **Watch body language.**
People may not be actively participating in a specific topic for a wide variety of reasons, both appropriate and inappropriate. For example, it may be OK if they don't have a strong opinion one way or the other, or the matter doesn't impact their area of responsibility. On the other hand, they may be silent because they are not fully familiar with the issue, are intimidated by the rank or personality of another speaker, or are preoccupied with another issue.

The Facilitator should watch how people react to others' comments.

The Facilitator should watch how people react to others' comments but avoid telegraphing judgments about their motivations and opinions. When you have body language clues about needs for greater participation, here are some approaches that can draw people out:

- "Jessica, we haven't heard from you on this as yet, and you look like you may have some questions. Is there something that needs clarification?"

- "Phil, as a front line person, does this characterize what you face every day? Do you think the solution will work for you as stated or does it need something more?" (to draw out lower ranking people)

- "Gerry, I know that you have a plane to catch right after this session and may have to leave early, so I want to be sure we don't miss your view. Are you ready to give us your thoughts?"

◆ **Discourage Domination.**
At times, you may face a situation where domination is obvious to all, and subtle intervention is not working. Here are some approaches that can effectively quiet the speaker without being overly offensive:

- In horseshoe and other layouts where the facilitator can move about, simply position yourself between the dominator and a person who has something to say and call on that person: "Jeannine, Chris has just given us a fairly comprehensive view on the subject from his perspective, but I believe the group would also like to hear from you and others."

- If your layout does not allow you to move, you may need to use hand gestures as well as eye contact and words to interrupt a monologue. With your hand up, you might say; "Chris, we have only 20 minutes for this item, and it's very important that we get input from others. I know that Al has been trying to get in for a while, so could we hear from him now?" Without waiting for a response from Chris, you turn to Al and say: "Al, your thoughts?"

- Another approach can both slow down the dominator and engage others that might not want to directly challenge the speaker. Get the group's attention (courteously but firmly interrupting the dominator if necessary) and take an approach like this: "Jan's got a very clear opinion on this; what I'd like to do in the next 5 to 10 minutes is form groups of three around the table and discuss what you've heard. When we come back to the main group, each trio can give a brief reaction to Jan's proposal and we'll see where that leads us."

  Alternately, if you don't want to use the break-out approach, you can refocus the group on the front of the room and ask that people take a minute or two to write down their thoughts on the matter to prepare for a broader discussion. When you reconvene use rotational input to get at least one comment from everyone around the table.

6

Take a Moment

Think about meetings that you have attended wherein participation was not what it should have been. In addition to the tips above, what techniques do you think could be effective in 1) drawing out the "silent sam" types, and 2) controlling people who tend to dominate?

_____

_____

_____

Staying on the Agenda

Good agenda planning, ensuring that time allocations for topics are realistic and match the desired outcomes, helps the meeting leader to stay on track. But, even diligent preparation won't cover all contingencies:

◆ Timely topics can capture the group's interest and cause loss of focus on the purpose and desired outcomes for the session.

◆ The world can change. Between the time the agenda was planned and the actual meeting, new data may become available or related meetings may have been conducted that change the direction of your desired outcomes.

Use a "Process Check" to Deal with Loss of Focus

The agenda and desired outcomes statements and your timekeeper and recorder are your best allies in this situation. Here's how to use the "process check" to get the group back on track:

◆ Look at your watch or ask your timekeeper to advise you regarding how much time you have spent on this item.

◆ Tell the group, "This is very interesting, but I believe that we may need to do a process check now," and quickly restate the desired outcome(s) for the topic you are working on.

◆ If the discussion does not appear to be supportive of the desired outcome, suggest that the subject be "parked" on a flip chart for further discussion after the desired outcomes have been achieved.

◆ Alternately, if the group feels strongly about the subject, you may offer to revise the agenda to drop something else in order to accommodate finishing the discussion. Either way, you have harnessed the group in support of staying on the agenda.

Handling New Information

You're well into your meeting and the group learns that new numbers have come out, or a fresh study has been published that materially impacts your work. This news immediately distracts from your agenda and puts your desired outcomes at risk. What do you do?

Nimble meeting leaders manage this sort of upset by revising the agenda and desired outcomes "on the fly". Here's an approach that will allow you to recover and get back on track with minimal wasted time:

◆ Signal a pause with a statement like: "I believe this new information really impacts what we were trying to do this morning, so let's stop for a minute or two to see if our agenda is still workable."

◆ Draw the group's attention to your purpose and desired outcomes statements, and get their input as to whether they are still appropriate or need tailoring.

◆ Using the input, rewrite the agenda and desired outcomes as required, and allocate the time you have remaining to the highest leverage topics.

◆ Sometimes, the new data makes your original meeting plan totally unworkable, and you're missing people or other resources needed to move in the new direction. In this case, get the group's input on what's needed for a follow-up session and adjourn.

6

Self-Check: Chapter Six Review

Answers to the following questions appear on Page 104.

	True	False
1. Normal meeting management rules apply in a "Spread the Heat" meeting.	_____	_____
2. Changing the agenda sequence, the meeting facility and bringing in outsiders are all ways to get routine meetings out of ruts.	_____	_____
3. Monitoring talk time is a good way to assess participation.	_____	_____
4. Process checks can be used bring a meeting back onto the agenda.	_____	_____

Notes

6

Appendix *One*

Using Six Handy Forms

Appendix Contents

▶ Meeting Work Order

▶ Meeting Preparation Checklist

▶ Meeting Cost Estimator

▶ Meeting Announcement and Agenda

▶ Meeting Agreements and Assignments

▶ Meeting Evaluation

This section includes six handy forms to guide you through the process of planning and executing your meetings. While excellent meetings are not about paper, these instruments can help you conduct meetings more effectively and efficiently. They include:

◆ **Meeting Work Order**
Use this form to determine whether a meeting is the best method to use, and if so, to answer the reporter's questions on what, where, when, why, and so on.

◆ **Meeting Preparation Checklist**
Use this to step through the process and guide others who have supporting roles in either preparation or execution of the event.

- ◆ **Meeting Cost Estimator**
  Working through the cost structure before the session will help you evaluate whether or not to meet and will identify out-of-pocket costs associated with the session.

- ◆ **Meeting Announcement and Agenda**
  The agenda is the heart of the meeting management process—the place where your planning comes together and the guide for the meeting. Don't take shortcuts!

- ◆ **Meeting Agreements and Assignments**
  Using this form on a flip chart or as projected computer image during a meeting ensures that your agreements have clarity and buy-in. Recording the "who does what by when" seals commitments and sets up natural follow-up sequences.

- ◆ **Meeting Evaluation**
  Adapt this form to meet the needs of your session—you can use the topics listed to generate verbal feedback or provide paper for more detailed comments.

Meeting Work Order

Purpose and Desired Outcomes:

Time available to prepare:

Item	Considerations	Conclusion
Should we Meet?	1. Is a meeting the best method to accomplish your goals? 2. What is/are the direction(s) of communication? 3. What degree of interaction is needed? 4. What is the substance of communication? 5. What is the group size you need to work with?	
What will it cost?	6. Use Meeting Cost Estimator Form to consider direct, indirect, and opportunity costs? 7. Is appropriate budget available?	
Where will we meet?	8. Select a layout from Chapter Three that meets the needs of the group and determine if an appropriate facility is available.	
When and for how long?	9. When are key stakeholders & participants available?	
Other Considerations		

Meeting Preparation Checklist

Item	Lead Responsibility	When Needed	Comments/ Special Considerations	Done?
Preparation Work				
Need a meeting or are other methods better?				
Define *purpose* and *desired outcomes*?				
Who should attend?			Travel arrangements for out-of-town people?	
RSVPs needed?				
When and where will the meeting be conducted?			Inspect ahead of time.	
What is the budget for the meeting?				
What materials and equipment are needed?			Review before meeting day.	
What room arrangement will work best?			Consider needs for interaction; sight lines for visual aids.	
What prework assignments should accompany the meeting notice?				
Who will present, facilitate, record, etc.? Is coffee or food service needed?			Rehearsal needed?	
Name tags or place cards needed ?			Place cards can control seating patterns even in groups that know each other.	

(continued on next page)

Meeting Preparation Checklist

Item	Lead Responsibility	When Needed	Comments/ Special Considerations	Done?
Meeting Day				
Who is to arrive early to check facility, equipment and materials?				
Start on time				
Stick to the agenda				
Evaluate				
Minutes/Notes published				

Meeting Cost Estimator

Item	Sample	Your Meeting
1. Number of people attending:	15	_____
2. Duration of meeting (hours)	2	_____
3. Average annual salary of people attending	$80,000	_____
4. Divide by 2000 to get average hourly cost	$40.00	_____
5. Multiple by number of people	X 15	_____
6. Hourly cost of group	$600	_____
7. Multiply by number of hours	X 2	_____
8. **Subtotal (direct salary costs)**	$1200	_____
9. Travel & lodging for out of towners	-	_____
10. Travel time costs for participants not on-site.	-	_____
11. Advance preparation time (meeting leader and administrative assistants)	$200	_____
12. Meeting room/meals/materials & support services	$100	_____
13. Opportunity costs (lost production or sales)	-	_____
Grand Total	$1500	_____

Meeting Announcement and Agenda

Subject/Purpose:

Called by:

Place:

Day/Date:	Time:	Duration:
Facilitator:	Recorder:	Timekeeper:

Participants:

Desired Outcomes

Order of Agenda

What	Who	How	Time

Meeting Agreements and Assignments

Agreements

Who: Lead Responsibility	What: Assignment	When: Timing

Meeting Evaluation

Results
(Achievement of Desired Outcomes)

Positives (+)	Opportunities to Improve (-)

Process
(How we achieved results)

Positives (+)	Opportunities to Improve (-)

Ratings
(5=Great; 1=Lots of Improvement Needed)

Results Rating	5	4	3	2	1
Process Rating	5	4	3	2	1
Overall Rating	5	4	3	2	1

Name (Optional) : _____

Notes

Appendix*Two*

Troubleshooting and Special Situations

Appendix Contents

▶ Anticipate and avoid common problems.

▶ Deal with special situations.

Working with Murphy's Law.

Even the best meeting managers aren't immune to *Murphy's Law*—"If something can go wrong, it will." Following is a table listing things that can go wrong during a meeting along with suggestions for avoiding them and resolving them when they do occur. The list isn't exhaustive, and the skilled meeting leader knows to expect the unexpected.

Troubleshooting Common Problems

Item	Issue	How to Avoid or Resolve
Beepers and cellular phones	Phones and pagers can be very distracting to the group, and can remove key stakeholders at inopportune times.	Some people may not be sensitive to this issue; it doesn't hurt to include a ground rule covering these.
Breaks	If you don't schedule breaks about every 90 minutes, people will license themselves to leave and disrupt your meeting.	Put breaks on your agenda and review them at the outset. Most people will hang in if they know that a break is coming and will be taken at or near the scheduled time.
Bullying	A group member may try to control another member with statements such as, *"You should do it that way,"* or *"You ought to stop that."*	Facilitators need to be on guard for language and statements that are perceived as attacks or threatening, and intervene by asking that offensive statements be reconsidered or rephrased.
Denigration	A group member may try to denigrate another member with statements that suggest that the speaker is right and the other person is stupid.	Facilitators need to jump in when questions like *"How could you possibly think that?"* emerge.
Digression	Topics or ideas that emerge unexpectedly and are interesting but off-track relative your purpose.	Get input from the group on whether to "park" the matter or to revise the agenda to accommodate the discussion.

Item	Issue	How to Avoid or Resolve
Food and Beverage Service	• Meetings involving food and beverage service can be inhibited instead of being enhanced if insufficient attention is paid to the details. • The skilled meeting planner will know the participants and the needs of the meeting when planning food and beverage services.	1. Consider age and lifestyles of participants when selecting beverages – in addition to coffee and tea, it's now common to offer juices and bottled water for morning sessions. Afternoon breaks need to include non-carbonated, caffeine-free and sugar-free choices in addition to traditional beverages. 2. Fruit and fat-free baked goods now typically are included in morning spreads, but some participants may prefer more traditional donuts and rolls. 3. Deli spreads with a variety of choices of fillers and condiments that allow people to make their own sandwich for lunch are safe (but potentially boring!), especially with salad makings as an alternate. Keep in mind that "make-it-yourself" takes more time than say, box lunches, and you'll need to allow for this in your agenda planning.
Heating, Ventilating and Air Conditioning	• HVAC issues have ruined many a meeting by creating problems in a room relative to temperature, noise, and lack of air movement	1. The skilled meeting planner knows the facility and arrives early to assure that everything is set correctly.

Item	Issue	How to Avoid or Resolve
Heating, Ventilating and Air Conditioning		2. Rooms warm up with people, so the meeting leader needs to know where the controls are or who to summon if the temperature is not appropriate. 3. Noise issues, coupled with room acoustics can be a substantial problem – if there's any doubt about being able to be heard, plan to use a PA system with roving microphones if appropriate.
Lecterns	Lecterns (called podiums by some) in public meeting facilities are notorious for being too tall or too short and for missing light bulbs for the reading light	• Check out the speaker's position in advance. • Unless the speaker needs to read word-for-word from a script, the use of lecterns is usually a bad idea as it isolates the speaker from the group. Use a clip-on microphone and a table for notes when possible.
Lighting	Common lighting problems include: • Room lighting washes out projected images. • Task lighting is too bright or dim. • Lighting controls in the don't provide adequate flexibility.	• Especially in hotels and other outside facilities, it's vital to check the room in advance to identify the potential issue. • A washed out screen can usually be eliminated or mitigated by careful placement of the screen, and if necessary, unscrewing lightbulbs in the immediate area.

Item	Issue	How to Avoid or Resolve
Lighting		• Many lighting issues simply can't be corrected, so the best bet is to chose another room or understand that you will have to work around some of the limitations.
Misrepresentation	A participant's statements indicate problems with facts and truth	• When you sense misrepresentation in a participant's commentary, you need to carefully coax your group to get at the truth. • Naïve questions can sometimes gently prod people into a more candid approach without creating the flinch that would be generated by a direct interrogation.
Name Tags and Place Cards	• Absence of name tags and place cards (or illegible ones), and failure to introduce participants is a common problem	• Examples are shown below.

Not-so-good Name Tag

Good Name Tag

Hello My Name Is

Mary Smith

Process Integration
Team *Mary*

Smith

Item	Issue	How to Avoid or Resolve
Rubber band	Refers to the need to bring members of the group up to speed on issues that have been discussed in prior sessions when some members were absent.	• Good documentation—meeting minutes or notes—that includes rationale for decisions goes a long way to eliminating this problem. Promptly published meeting results, along with a group norm to read the notes, will minimize this concern. • Even with good documentation, you can still revisit or reopen an issue if the member who was absent has strong beliefs about it. • All need to be patient with this process, as all people don't absorb information at the same rate or in the same way.
Screens	Some of the best first hotels do not understand the need for good projection screens of sufficient size to handle overheads in a small meeting room.	• Understand what size screen(s) you need and make arrangements with the meeting facility or a rental agency. • Arrive early to ensure you have what you need and have a back-up plan in case you are disappointed with what the facility has.
Selling past the close	Allowing discussion on a topic to continue after agreement has been reached.	When you've reached agreement, confirm it and move on to avoid reopening the discussion and risking an unraveling of the agreement.

Item	Issue	How to Avoid or Resolve
Sight lines	• Even in smaller meetings, inattention to room layout can create problems for participants in terms of sight lines to screens and flip charts. • When people can't see the visuals, their participation will be limited, and their mood is likely to be less than fully supportive.	• When designing visual aids (overheads and projected presentations) use large font sizes (20 point or larger) in combination with large screens to assure legibility. • Flip chart operators should use bold markers and print using large and legible characters.
Tape and Markers	• The first page of group memory comes off the flip chart and the recorder doesn't have tape to hang the output, and/or his/her marker runs dry and there are no more in sight.	• Don't leave home without a good supply of bold markers in a variety of colors, as well as masking tape for use in hanging flip chart sheets on the wall.

Special Situations -- When To Throw Out The Rules

There are times when the experienced participants or leaders will recognize that normal meeting guidelines either shouldn't or won't be followed, and will accept a less-than completely organized session. Two are discussed briefly below:

Item	Issue	How to Avoid or Resolve
Meeting after the Meeting	• Ad-hoc sessions, typically convened by the senior person or other key stakeholders, to "interpret" the outcomes of the meeting and provide commentary on the proceedings.	• For the leader of preceding session, listen carefully and take notes. You will get information that the boss or others did not want to share in the open session. • This may relate to the outcomes of the formal meeting and can be very important –perceptions about the strength of agreements, or next steps. • It can also include items of career importance about how the meeting was planned or conducted, such little things like, "Next time, let's select a facility without a noisy kitchen."
Wallowing	• Loosely controlled discussion; one step up from a free form bull session and, unlike formal brainstorming, there is such a thing as a dumb idea. Typically used early in group work on a new topic, or at a point when the group seems to be stymied. With time limited for these discussions, they can be productive in generating breakthrough ideas to solve knotty issues.	• Limit the time and the subject matter, but otherwise let the discussion flow in free and if appropriate, passionate form. • Do maintain courtesy and protect people from personal attacks. It doesn't hurt to pull comments out of people who are quiet. • Group memory (flip charts) often get generated spontaneously and may be useful later in constructing formal rationale. Don't throw paper away until you're sure it's not needed!

Special Situations

Flag System for Facilitator Support by Participants

While the facilitator has overall responsibility for meeting pacing and control, participants can provide considerable assistance. Participant support is especially important in larger group meetings and those wherein the facilitator may not have clear sight lines to all participants.

Skilled facilitators, working with familiar people in smaller groups, don't usually need the formal support of participants, as they can read the verbal and non-verbal signals they need from the group. However, with less familiar or larger groups, even the best facilitators can improve the effectiveness and efficiency of their sessions using a flag system, such as the one described below.

The system can provide the facilitator with important information on a timely basis with minimal risk of inappropriate interruption. Each participant is provided with a set of 3" x 5" (or larger) cards that function as "flags" to draw the facilitators attention, with color coding as follows:

- **Green:** We're moving in the right direction and making progress, but we can (or need to) pick up the pace.

- **Red:** Meeting is off track (digressions) or there is questionable progress toward desired outcomes—need to stop and assess, facilitator intervention required ASAP.

- **Yellow:** I need to interrupt—facilitator please call on me. (May be an important but off-subject matter that needs to be noted for later discussion, an observation (aha!) or a need for an unscheduled break.)

- **Blue/White (Divers Flag):** Discussion is more involved or detailed than needed to achieve desired outcome ("Depth of Dive" is too deep). Prompt action on the part of the facilitator is needed to move discussion to a different forum or obtain group permission to adjust time frames and continue.

- **Checkered:** We've achieved our desired outcome(s); it's time to adjourn or move on to the next item.

In groups that meet on a recurring basis, the need for physical "flags" will diminish quickly. Regular participants familiar with the code will call out the appropriate color or use non-verbal cues to signal the facilitator with his or her suggestion.

Answers to Chapter Reviews

Chapter One

1. Just a <u>10 percent</u> reduction in time spent in meetings would result in substantial savings for organizations and improved work life for employees.

2. For many in the workplace today, time has become <u>more</u> valuable than money.

3. Results needed
   Type of work to be done
   Costs associated with the meeting
   Alternative methods available

4. Choose from:
   Conference calls
   Web- or LAN-based on-line meetings
   Videotaped messages
   Paper or e-mail bulletins with response mechanisms
   Studies conducted by individuals
   Documents created collaboratively

5. Critical mass means that you have to have enough people that "know the rules" of meeting management in order to get started, and have some degree of management support.

6. Meeting management is about achieving desired outcomes, not getting done in an hour regardless of results. Too stringent enforcement of rules at the expense of accomplishments can be counter productive.

Chapter Two

1. *Why* are you holding the meeting?
   What do you want to accomplish?
   Who should participate?
   How should you conduct the meeting?
   When should you hold the meeting, and how long should it take?

2. *Purpose statements* are short, punchy phrases that typically describe the <u>subject matter</u> content of a meeting. *Desired outcomes statements* are longer and more specific— they describe the <u>actual work</u> to be done during the session.

3. True: Generally speaking, a smaller group size is better if a high degree of interaction is needed.

4. Choose from:
   Presentation
   Present and discuss
   Q & A
   Brainstorm
   Consolidate
   Order/Prioritize
   Develop
   Agree
   Evaluate
   Recap

5. List desired outcomes near the top of the page or next to topics.

6. When meeting participants already know each other.

Chapter Three

1. Choose from:
   Group size
   Location
   Interaction
   Control
   Power
   Media
   Privacy and quiet
   Availability

2. b. Oval or rectangle

3. c. Small Theater

4. a. Classroom

5. c. Theater seating.

Chapter Four

Advanced Method	Benefit
1. Choosing logical sequences for your meeting.	Tailors your subject matter to the meeting situation.
2. Using the Stakeholder Analysis method for participant selection	Allows a logical approach to inviting people to a meeting based on the desired outcomes and the nature of the subject matter.
3. Using Political Mapping	Provides a way to analyze the positions held by various potential participants in the context of their influence on the situation.
4. Using the *Three Dimensional Outline*™ meeting preparation	Provides a very comprehensive look at preparations needed for important meetings.

Chapter Five

	True	False
1. A good meeting leader can conduct an excellent meeting without understanding the desired outcomes.	_____	X
2. You can save time at the outset of the meeting by getting directly to the task.	_____	X
3. Role assignments aren't important when the leader is the facilitator and recorder.	_____	X

4. Though consistency is important; skilled facilitators will pacing or approach when the situation warrants. X _____

5. Involvement of all isn't important as long as you get to the answer you're seeking. _____ X

6. Evaluations should focus clearly on the results of the session. _____ X

7. Timekeepers should interrupt presenters if they have run over heir allotted time _____ X

8. The preferred form of follow-up documentation is the timed work plan. X _____

9. Informal documentation is OK when the need for buy-in by non-participants is low. X _____

Chapter Six

	True	False
1. Normal meeting management rules apply in a "Spread the Heat" meeting.	_____	X
2. Changing the agenda sequence, the meeting facility and bringing in outsiders are all ways to get routine meetings out of ruts.	X	_____
3. Monitoring talk time is a good way to assess participation.	X	_____
4. Process checks can be used bring a meeting back onto the agenda.	X	_____